Math in Focus™

The Singapore Approach

Enrichment

2A

Consultant and Author
Dr. Fong Ho Kheong

Author
Ang Kok Cheng

Marshall Cavendish
Education

GREAT SOURCE
HOUGHTON MIFFLIN HARCOURT
Supplemental Publishers

© 2009 Marshall Cavendish International (Singapore) Private Limited

Published by Marshall Cavendish Education
An imprint of Marshall Cavendish International (Singapore) Private Limited
A member of Times Publishing Limited

Marshall Cavendish International (Singapore) Private Limited
Times Centre, 1 New Industrial Road
Singapore 536196
Tel: +65 6411 0820
Fax: +65 6266 3677
E-mail: fps@sg.marshallcavendish.com
Website: www.marshallcavendish.com/education

Distributed by
Great Source
A division of Houghton Mifflin Harcourt Publishing Company
181 Ballardvale Street
P.O. Box 7050
Wilmington, MA 01887-7050
Tel: 1-800-289-4490
Website: www.greatsource.com

First published 2009
Reprinted 2010

Math in Focus ™ is a trademark of Times Publishing Limited.

Great Source ® is a registered trademark of Houghton Mifflin Harcourt Publishing Company.

Math in Focus Enrichment 2A
ISBN 978-0-669-01577-5

Printed in Singapore

2 3 4 5 6 7 8   1897   16 15 14 13 12 11 10
4500229728   B C D E

Contents

Introducing

Math in Focus™

Enrichment

Written to complement *Math in Focus™: The Singapore Approach* Grade 2, exercises in *Enrichment 2A* and *2B* are designed for advanced students seeking a challenge beyond the exercises and questions in the Student Books and Workbooks.

These exercises require children to draw on their fundamental mathematical understanding as well as recently acquired concepts and skills, combining problem-solving strategies with critical thinking skills.

Critical thinking skills enhanced by working on *Enrichment* exercises include classifying, comparing, sequencing, analyzing parts and whole, identifying patterns and relationships, induction (from specific to general), deduction (from general to specific), and spatial visualization.

One set of problems is provided for each chapter, to be assigned after the chapter has been completed. *Enrichment* exercises can be assigned while other students are working on the Chapter Review/Test, or while the class is working on subsequent chapters.

CHAPTER 1 Numbers to 1,000

PROBLEM SOLVING
Thinking Skills

Answer these questions.
Show your work.

1.   Five teams take part in a quiz show.
     Their scores are shown.
     Order their scores from least to greatest.
     Then fill in the blanks.

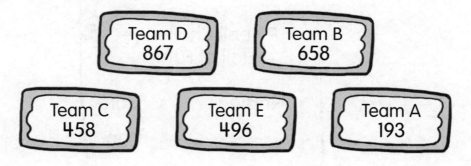

Team D
867

Team B
658

Team C
458

Team E
496

Team A
193

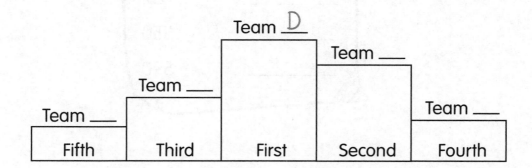

Team _D_

Team ___

Team ___

Team ___

Team ___

Fifth   Third   First   Second   Fourth

2.   Five children play a game of pinball.
How many points does each of them score?
Read the clues.
Then fill in the blanks.

Clues

- Kelly scores 590 points.
- Steven comes in last.
- Tammy scores 100 points less than 930.
- Gina misses a shot worth 100 points, so she does not score 650 points.
- Elle is one of the players.

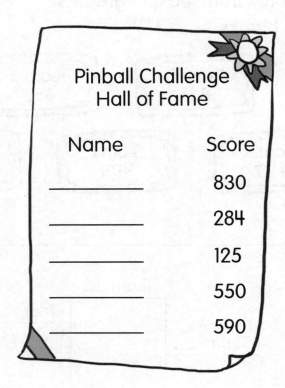

Pinball Challenge
Hall of Fame

Name	Score
_____	830
_____	284
_____	125
_____	550
_____	590

Form three-digit numbers.

Circle three digits horizontally (←, →),

vertically (↓, ↑), or diagonally (↙, ↘, ↗, ↖).

Example

Which is the greatest number that is less than 1,000?

3	6	4
5	9	2
7	8	1

The number is 896.

---

3.   Which is the least number that is greater than 100?

5	6	2
4	1	7
9	8	3

---

4.   Add the digits of each three-digit number.
The total is greater than 15 but less than 20.
Which number is it?

5	6	2
4	1	7
9	8	3

PROBLEM SOLVING
Strategies

Fill in the blanks.
Use base-ten blocks to help you.

5.   245 is 45 more than _____.

6.   3 tens less than 4 hundreds is _____.

7.   8 hundreds is _____ more than 40 tens.

Complete the number patterns.

8.

464		
504		

374		474			674

| 564 |
| 584 |

Solve.

9.   Leslie draws shapes to show some numbers.

275	♡♡ ☆☆☆ ◯◯
175	♡ ☆☆ ◯
75	☆

Draw a similar set of shapes to show 375.

| 375 | |

10.   Which number does not belong in this group?
Color the box that has the number that does not belong.

347   129

246   358   729

PROBLEM SOLVING
Exploration

Answer these questions.
Show your work.

11. Write all the three-digit numbers you can make using these digits.

_____

_____

_____

_____

12. The greatest three-digit number is _____.

13. The least three-digit number is _____.

14. Dana has six cards with a number written on each card.
The numbers can be arranged to form a pattern.
What can the numbers on the two remaining cards be?
Show three different sets of patterns that Dana can form
using the cards.

| 750 | 850 | 700 | 800 | ? | ? |

Pattern 1

Pattern 2

Pattern 3

Journal Writing

Explain the steps.

15. Order the numbers from least to greatest.

287 496 469 99

Number the steps correctly.
Write 1, 2, 3, or 4 in the boxes.

☐ Compare the hundreds of the three remaining numbers. The number with the least hundreds digit is next.

☐ The remaining number is greatest.

☐ Compare the tens of the two remaining numbers that have the same hundreds.
The number with less tens is next.

☐ Compare the number of digits in each number.
The number with fewer than three digits is least.

Least ─ ☐ ─ ☐ ─ ☐ ─ ☐ ─→ Greatest

16. Order the numbers from least to greatest.

472 507 88 540

Explain the steps you use to compare the numbers.
Then fill in the blanks.

Step 1 _____

_____

Step 2 _____

_____

Step 3 _____

_____

Step 4 _____

_____

Least → [ ] [ ] [ ] [ ] → Greatest

Correct the mistakes.
Write the correct sentences.

17.   75 more than 475 is 400.

_____

_____

18.   125 less than 525 is 650.

_____

_____

19.   These numbers make a number pattern.

274   375   476   567   499

_____

_____

20.   These numbers are ordered from least to greatest.

370   99   901   307   299

_____

_____

CHAPTER 2 Addition up to 1,000

PROBLEM SOLVING
Thinking Skills

Solve.
Show your work.

1.   Color the two eggs that have numbers that add up to 528.

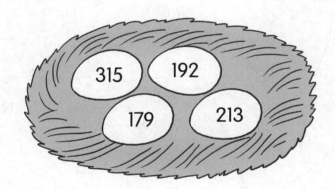

2.   Color the three eggs that have numbers that add up to 394.

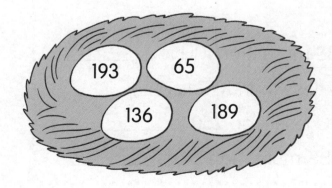

3. Ian wants to unlock a safe but he cannot remember his code.
He has some clues to help him find the code.

a. Complete the clues.
Use the code wheel to help you.

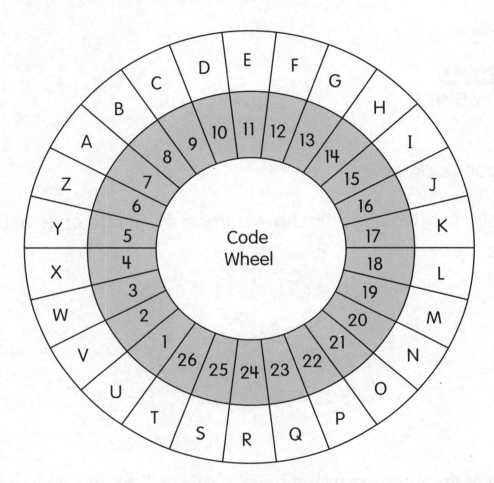

M = 19, U = 1
MU = 191

Clues

Digit 1: 238 more than MU is _____.

Digit 2: JZ less than XYZ is _____.

Digit 3: GU less than 250 is _____.

Digit 4: ABC more than HC is _____.

b. Circle the four-digit code on the safe.
Use the answers in Exercise 3a and the translator
to help you.

Translator

0 → 119	1 → 912	2 → 236	3 → 938
4 → 587	5 → 429	6 → 246	7 → 593
8 → 290	9 → 394		

The code is _____.

Solve.
Show your work.

4. Mrs. Thomas has $400 to decorate her living room.
    Help her spend as much of her money to buy as many different
    items as possible.
    Circle the items that she can buy.

bookcase   couch   chair

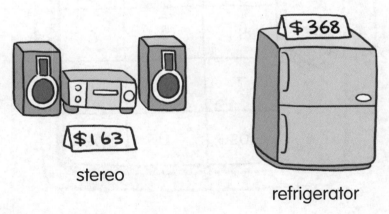

stereo

refrigerator

PROBLEM SOLVING
Strategies

Fill in the missing numbers.

5.

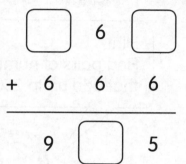

```
    ☐    6    ☐
 +  6    6    6
 ─────────────────
    9    ☐    5
```

6.

```
    ☐    5    9
 +  4   ☐    ☐
 ─────────────────
    9    4    8
```

Name: _____ **Date:** _____

Solve.
Show your work.

7. Add these numbers.

55 75 95 115 135 155 175

Hint:
Find pairs of numbers
that add up to 250.

8. Mrs. Parker sells 192 bookmarks on Monday.
She sells 163 more bookmarks on Tuesday than on Monday.
She has 34 bookmarks left.
How many bookmarks did Mrs. Parker have at first?

Mrs. Parker had _____ bookmarks at first.

9.   Samantha gives 80 seashells to her cousin.
She gives 72 seashells to her brother.
She drops 145 seashells into a drain.
There are 69 seashells left.
How many seashells did Samantha have at first?

Samantha had _____ seashells at first.

10.   Jack has some baseball cards.
Kathy and Lionel do not have any cards.
Jack gives some cards to Kathy.
Jack has 127 cards left.
Kathy gives some cards to Lionel.
Kathy has 289 cards left.
Lionel now has 358 cards.
How many baseball cards did Jack have at first?

Jack had _____ baseball cards at first.

PROBLEM SOLVING
Exploration

Solve.
Show your work.

11. Find the path of numbers that gives the greatest sum.
    Trace the path in red.
    What is the greatest sum?

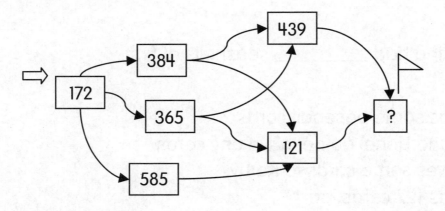

The greatest sum is _____.

Fill in the missing numbers.

12.

$$
\begin{array}{r}
4\ \boxed{}\ 6 \\
+\ 3\ \boxed{}\ 7 \\
\hline
8\ 0\ 3
\end{array}
$$

Journal Writing

Correct the mistakes.
Write the correct answers.

13.
```
   1 3 7
 + 4 8 6
 -------
   5 1 3
```

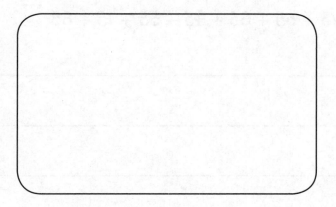

14.
```
   5 7 2
 + 3 4 5
 -------
   8 1 8
```

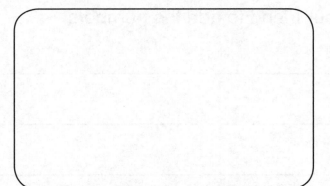

Solve.

15. Andy uses a pattern to add these numbers.
Write down the pattern he uses.
Then add the numbers.

25 + 75 + 65 + 35 + 45 + 55 + 15 + 85

_____

_____

_____

_____

_____

16. Write down six numbers that can be added using a pattern.
Ask your friend to add the numbers.

_____

_____

_____

_____

_____

CHAPTER 3 Subtraction up to 1,000

PROBLEM SOLVING
Thinking Skills

Fill in the blanks.

1.   332 + _____ = 563

2.   _____ + 310 = 893

3.   42 + _____ = 236

4.   _____ + 289 = 608

Complete the number puzzle.

5.

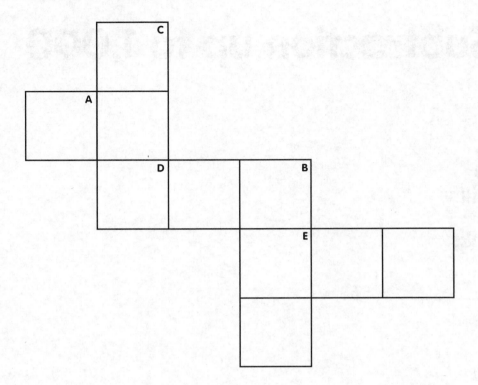

Down

B: _____ is 238 more than 201.

C: 150 less that 603 is _____.

Across

A: 425 – 360 = _____.

D: 154 is _____ less than 538.

E: 728 – _____ = 364.

Solve.
Show your work.

6.   Fraser has 68 stickers.
Peter gives Fraser some stickers.
Kelly gives Fraser 48 stickers.
Fraser now has 131 stickers.
How many stickers did Peter give Fraser?

Peter gave Fraser _____ stickers.

7.   A box contains 736 colored bands.
249 of the bands are yellow.
There are 150 fewer red bands than yellow bands.
The remaining bands are blue.
How many blue bands does the box contain?

The box contains _____ blue bands.

PROBLEM SOLVING
Strategies

Fill in the missing numbers.

8.

```
  [ ]    8    [ ]

–  4   [ ]   9
_____
   3    6    7
```

```
┌─────────── Example ───────────────────────────────────┐
│                                                         │
│                  ┌────────┐                             │
│                  │   79   │                             │
│         ┌────────┼────────┼────────┐                    │
│         │  180   │   76   │  256   │                    │
│         └────────┼────────┼────────┘                    │
│                  │  155   │                             │
│                  └────────┘                             │
│                                                         │
└─────────────────────────────────────────────────────────┘
```

Each set of numbers follows a pattern.

9.

```
                  ┌────────┐
                  │        │
         ┌────────┼────────┼────────┐
         │  867   │        │  783   │
         └────────┼────────┼────────┘
                  │  155   │
                  └────────┘
```

Fill in the missing numbers.

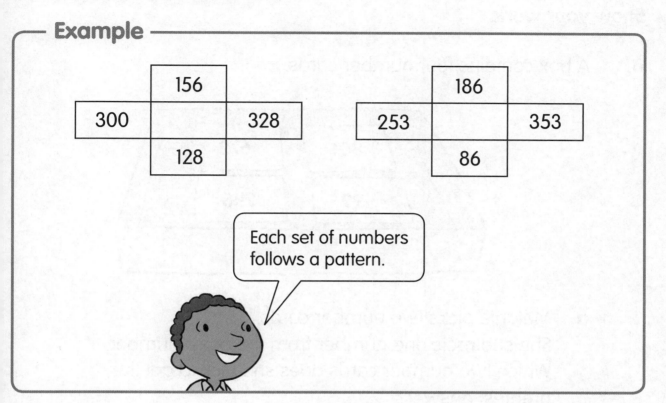

Example

156
300   328
128

186
253   353
86

Each set of numbers follows a pattern.

10.

295
183   235
?

The missing number is _____.

Solve.
Show your work.

11.   A box contains four number cards.

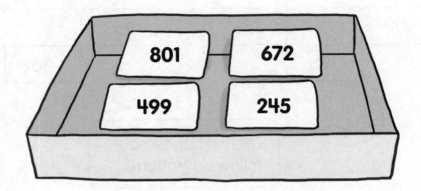

a.   Melanie picks two number cards.
She subtracts one number from the other number.
Which two number cards does she pick to get the
greatest answer?

b.   Melanie puts back the two number cards.
Jessie takes out two number cards and subtracts one
number from the other.
Which two numbers does Jessie pick to get the least
answer?

12.   Some fish are in a pond.
Mr. Hogan adds 156 guppies into the pond.
Two days later, he adds 85 goldfish and 95 swordtails.
There are now 495 fish in the pond.
How many fish were in the pond at first?

_____ fish were in the pond at first.

Exploration

Fill in the blanks.

13. Regroup 6 hundreds in different ways.

6 hundreds = ___5___ hundreds ___10___ tens ___0___ ones

= _____ hundreds _____ tens _____ ones

= _____ hundreds _____ tens _____ ones

14. Find all possible values of digits X and Y.
Write your answers in the table.

```
   8  0  7
−  5 [X] 5
───────────
   2 [Y] 2
```

X	Y

Name: _____ **Date:** _____

 **Journal Writing**

Solve.
Show your work.

15. Lee and Sue are playing a game.
Lee gives Sue 84 marbles, Sue returns 39 marbles to Lee.
Lee gives Sue 56 marbles, Sue returns 11 marbles to Lee.
Lee gives Sue 73 marbles, Sue returns 28 marbles to Lee.

a. Explain the rule for the number pattern used in the game.

_____

_____

b. Lee gives Sue 100 marbles.
How many marbles does Sue return to Lee?

Sue returns _____ marbles to Lee.

c. Sue returns 90 marbles to Lee.
How many marbles did Lee give Sue?

Lee gave Sue _____ marbles.

16. Write the three steps used to subtract 328 from 700.

$$
\begin{array}{r}
700 \\
-\ 328 \\
\hline
\end{array}
$$

Step 1 _____

_____

_____

Step 2 _____

_____

_____

Step 3 _____

_____

_____

CHAPTER 4

Using Bar Models: Addition and Subtraction

PROBLEM SOLVING
Strategies

Solve.
Use the bar models to help you.

1.   Sally has 85 stamps.
      Mary has 29 stamps fewer than Sally.
      Mary gives away 15 stamps.
      How many stamps does Mary have in the end?

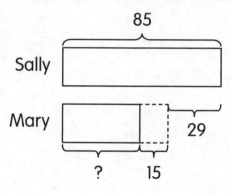

      Mary has _____ stamps in the end.

2. 59 people buy tickets to a show.
46 of them buy tickets to stall seats.
37 of them buy tickets to gallery seats.
How many people buy tickets for both stall seats and gallery seats?

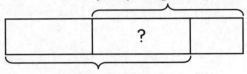

37 people (gallery seats)

?

46 people (stall seats)

_____ people buy tickets for both stall seats and gallery seats.

3. At a fundraiser, Matthew sells 450 more pencils than Jenny.
Lily sells 425 more pencils than Jenny.
Matthew sells 875 pencils.
How many pencils does Lily sell?

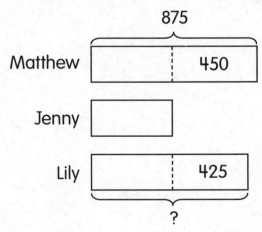

875

Matthew   450

Jenny

Lily   425

?

Lily sells _____ pencils.

4. For a charity drive, Jason collects 43 more toys than Tom.
Tom collects 12 fewer toys than Nick.
Nick collects 32 toys.
How many toys do the three children collect in all?

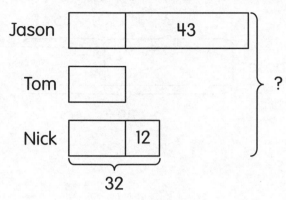

They collect _____ toys in all.

5. Chelsea has some strawberries.
She throws 12 rotten strawberries away.
She buys another 35 strawberries.
She now has 84 strawberries.
How many strawberries did Chelsea have at first?

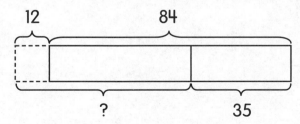

Chelsea had _____ strawberries at first.

6. Adrian has some packets of pasta and cheese.
He exchanges 5 packets of pasta for 35 packets of cheese.
He now has 41 packets of pasta and 89 packets of cheese.
How many packets of pasta and cheese did Adrian have at first?

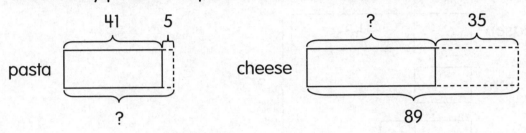

Adrian had _____ packets of pasta and cheese at first.

7. Mike has 104 more stamps than Nicole.
He gives some stamps to Nicole.
They now have the same number of stamps.
Nicole now has 180 stamps.
How many stamps did Mike have at first?

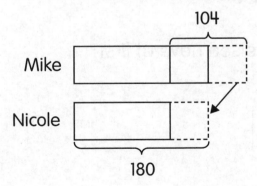

Mike had _____ stamps at first.

PROBLEM SOLVING
Exploration

Write a real-world problem for each bar model.

8.

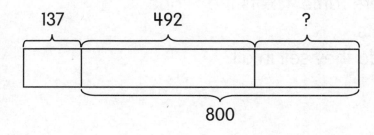

137   492   ?

800

_____

_____

_____

_____

9.

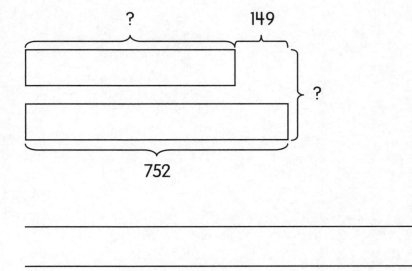

?   149

?

752

_____

_____

_____

_____

 **Journal Writing**

**Correct the mistakes in the bar model.
Then solve.**

10.   Lincoln sells 128 more raffle tickets than Jane.
Jane sells 300 tickets.
How many tickets do they sell in all?

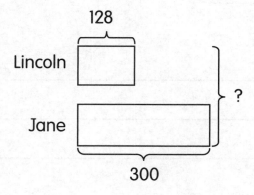

They sell _____ tickets in all.

Solve.
Show your work.
Use the bar model to help you.

11.   Terry has 560 books.
Linda has 125 fewer books than Terry.
How many books do they have in all?

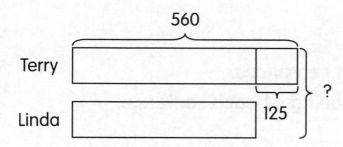

They have _____ books in all.

CHAPTER 5 Multiplication and Division

PROBLEM SOLVING

Thinking Skills

Complete the multiplication sentences.

Draw ◯s to show the meaning of each sentence.

1.   5 × 7 = _____

   7 × 5 = _____

What is the difference between the two multiplication sentences?

_____

_____

Color all the values that are equal.

2.

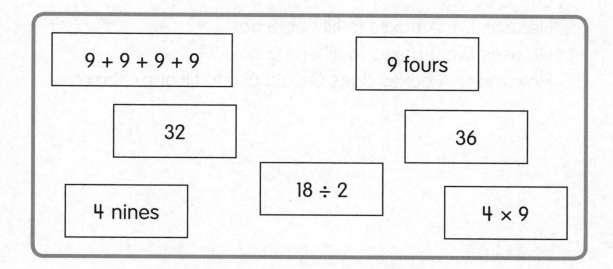

Solve.
Show your work.

3. Four A boxes fill a B box.
Four B boxes fill a C box.
How many A boxes fill a C box?

| A |

| B |

| C |

_____ A boxes fill a C box.

4.   Gerald has boxes of three different sizes: A boxes, B boxes, and C boxes.

He uses five A boxes to fill one B box.

He uses five B boxes to fill one C box.

How many A boxes does Gerald use to fill one C box?

Gerald uses _____ A boxes to fill one C box.

PROBLEM SOLVING

Strategies

Fill in the blanks.

5. Complete the number pattern.

35, 28, 21, _____, 7

6. Use the numbers to form two multiplication sentences.
You do not need to use all the numbers.

2, 3, 6, 7, 8, 16, 21

_____ × _____ = _____

_____ × _____ = _____

7. ☆, ☾, and △ all represent different numbers.
☆ is less than ☾.

Find the number that each shape represents.

$$☆ × ☾ = 8 \qquad △ ÷ ☆ = 8$$

☆ = _____   ☾ = _____   △ = _____

Solve.
Show your work.

8. A farmer has 4 ducks, 3 chickens, and some cows.
    The animals have 30 legs in all.
    How many cows does the farmer have?

    The farmer has _____ cows.

9. Find the number that each fruit represents.

    🍎 ÷ 3 = 🍊

    🍊 × 6 = 🍐

    🍐 − 2 = 28

    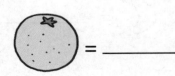 🍎 = _____   🍊 = _____   🍐 = _____

PROBLEM SOLVING

Exploration

Solve.
Show your work.

10. Sue puts 24 sheets of paper into some files.
Each file has an equal number of sheets.
How many ways can she divide the sheets of paper among
the files?
Write a multiplication and a division sentence for each way.

11. There are bicycles, tricycles, and cars in an open area.
There are 32 wheels in all.
How many bicycles, tricycles, and cars can there be?

Journal Writing

Solve and explain.

12. Write two sentences about each number sentence.

| 3 × 8 | _____ |

_____

| 12 ÷ 4 | _____ |

_____

13. Paul has two rabbits and some chickens.
The animals have 14 legs in all.
How many chickens does Paul have?
Explain your answer.

_____

_____

_____

_____

_____

CHAPTER 6

Multiplication Tables of 2, 5, and 10

PROBLEM SOLVING
Thinking Skills

Multiply.

Fill in the ☐ **s.**

1.

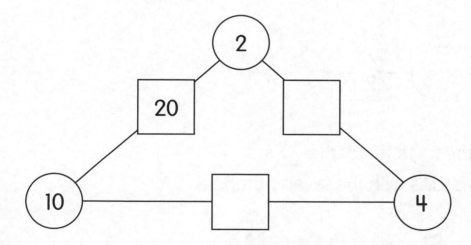

2.

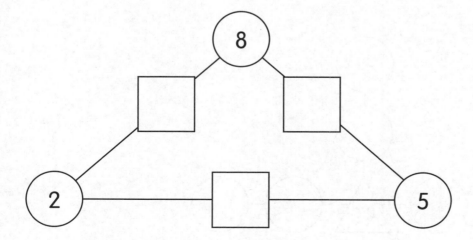

Fill in the missing numbers.
Use each number only once.

3.   Multiply the ◯s to get the △s.

Fill in the circles with the given numbers.

1   2   5   4   10   20

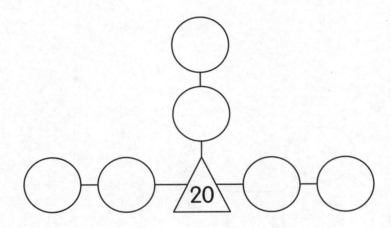

4.   Multiply the ◯s to get the △s.

Fill in the circles with the given numbers.

1   4   5   8   10   40

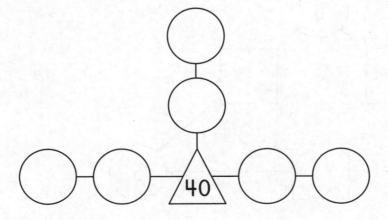

5. Multiply the ◯s to get the ☐s.
Fill in the circles with the given numbers.
Then fill in the squares.

2 4 5 10

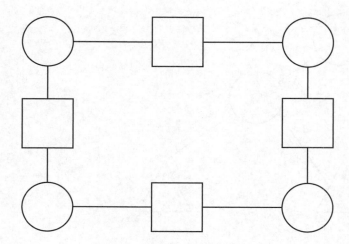

6. Multiply the ◯s to get the ☐s.
Fill in the circles with numbers that are greater than 1
and less than 10.
Then fill in the squares.

7. Multiply the △s.
Add the middle row of ◯s.
Use each number only once.

5 7 8 35 40 75

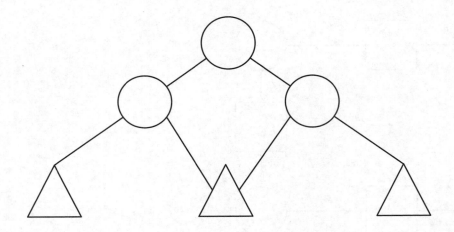

8. Multiply the △s.
Add the middle row of ◯s.
Use each number only once.

5 9 50 140 90 10

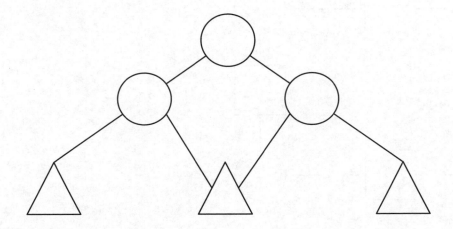

PROBLEM SOLVING

Strategies

One of the three numbers is put into the machine.
The machine produces the final number given.
Multiply and divide to fill in the missing numbers.

9.

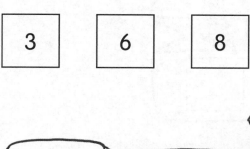

| 3 | 6 | 8 |

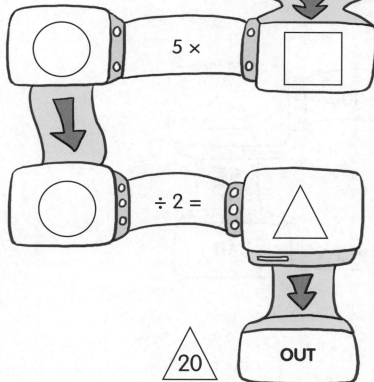

IN

5 ×

÷ 2 =

OUT

20

One of the three numbers is put into the machine.
The machine produces the final number given.
Multiply and divide to fill in the missing numbers.

10.

3   6   8

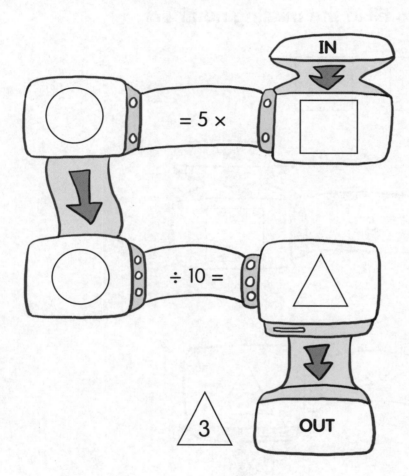

IN

= 5 ×

÷ 10 =

3

OUT

11. Multiply the ◯s to get the ▢s.
Fill in the circles with the given numbers.
You may use the given numbers more than once.
All the squares add up to 84.
Fill in the squares.

2 5 10

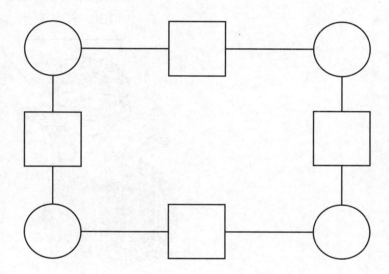

12. Complete the number pattern.

30, 12, 25, _____, 20, 8, 15, 6, _____, 4, 5, 2

Solve.
Show your work.

13. A train has 10 cars.
Each car is 10 meters long.
The cars are joined by links, each 2 meters long.
What is the length of the train?

Hint:
Draw a picture to
help you.

The length of the train is _____ meters.

PROBLEM SOLVING
Exploration

Look at the numbers.

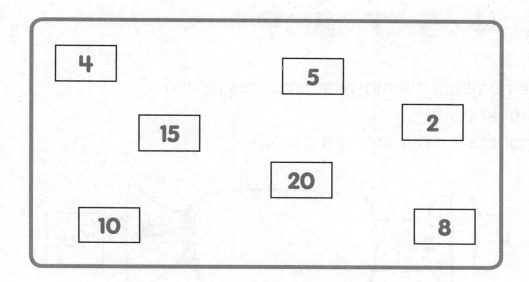

14. Shade all the numbers you can get by multiplying by 2.

15. Circle all the numbers you can get by multiplying by 5.

16. What numbers are both shaded and circled?

_____

17. Write down five numbers between 100 and 150.
Which of these five numbers would be both shaded and circled?

_____, _____, _____, _____, _____

_____

Solve.

18.   4 is put into the multiplication machine.
The machine produces 20.
Sam picks four numbers from these numbers.

3 4 5 7 8 9

The numbers the machine produces form a
number pattern.
What are the numbers produced?

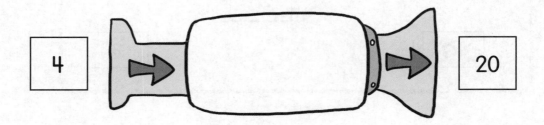

The numbers produced are _____, _____,

_____, and _____.

Journal Writing

Solve and explain.

19. Jennifer takes 24 beads from a bag.
She divides them equally into groups of 2.
She wants to divide the beads into equal groups of 5.
Can she divide the beads equally each time?
Explain why or why not.

_____

_____

_____

_____

_____

_____

_____

_____

_____

_____

_____

Correct the mistakes.

20. $7 \times 2 = 14$
There are 2 chickens.
The chickens have 14 legs in all.

_____

_____

_____

21. $9 \times 2 = 29$

_____

_____

_____

22. $7 \times 5 = 3 \times 5 + 2 \times 5$

_____

_____

_____

CHAPTER 7 Metric Measurement of Length

PROBLEM SOLVING
Thinking Skills

Look at the picture.
Fill in the blanks.

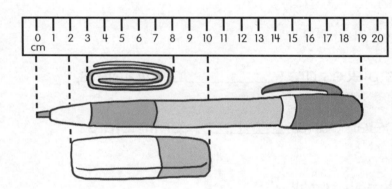

This ruler is smaller than in real life.

1.   The paper clip is _____ centimeters shorter than the pen.

2.   The eraser is _____ centimeters longer than the paper clip,

   but _____ centimeters shorter than the pen.

3.   If the three objects are placed in a straight line, what will the
   length of the line be?

   The line will be _____ centimeters long.

Solve.
Show your work.

4.   Sean makes a 100-centimeter rope by joining three pieces of
     rope together.
     What are the lengths of the pieces that he joins together?

25 cm	18 cm	60 cm
42 cm	75 cm	40 cm

The lengths of the pieces are _____ centimeters,

_____ centimeters, and _____ centimeters.

5.   Belinda is 90 centimeters tall.
     Raymond is 24 centimeters taller than Kate.
     Kate is 8 centimeters shorter than Belinda.
     What is the total height of Raymond and Kate?

Their total height is _____ centimeters.

PROBLEM SOLVING
Strategies

Fill in the blanks.

6.

| 90 m | − | ⬭ | + | 8 m | → | 10 m |

| 19 m | + | △ | − | 12 m | → | 10 m |

Solve.
Show your work.

7.   Mr. Denver builds three toy houses for his children.
Melvin's house is 15 centimeters taller than Betty's house.
Betty's house is 25 centimeters taller than Serene's house.
The total height of the three houses is 125 centimeters.
What is the height of Serene's house?

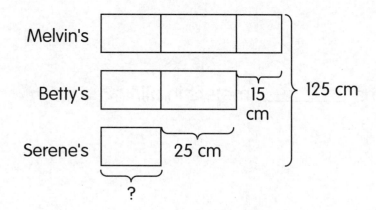

Serene's house is _____ centimeters tall.

8.   For every 5 meters that Ben swims up a river, he drifts 3 meters
back down the river.
Ben travels 12 meters up the river.
How many meters does Ben swim?

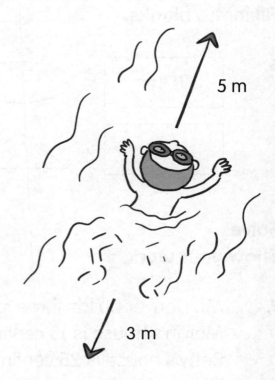

Ben swims _____ meters in all.

9. Mr. Foster places 11 garden lights along an 80-meter path.
Each light is placed an equal distance apart.
How far away is the sixth garden light from the second?

0 m   80 m

The sixth garden light is _____ meters away from the
second.

10. Two pieces of wood are glued together.
One piece is twice as long as the other.
The total length of the glued wood is 250 centimeters.
What is the length of the shorter piece of wood?

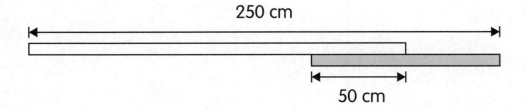

250 cm

50 cm

The shorter piece of wood is _____ centimeters long.

PROBLEM SOLVING

Exploration

Solve.

Show your work.

11. Write two different ways to find out how much longer the eraser is than the paper clip.

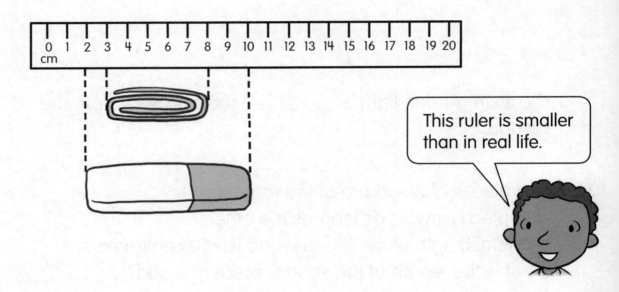

This ruler is smaller than in real life.

12. The figure shows six small rectangles that form a big rectangle. Each small rectangle has a length of 15 centimeters and a width of 12 centimeters.

A snail crawls from A to B along the straight lines.

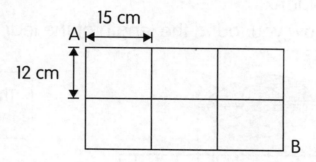

What is the shortest distance the snail can crawl?

The shortest distance the snail can crawl is _____ centimeters.

Journal Writing

Solve and explain.

13.   Fill in the blank.
       Explain how you found the length of the leaf.

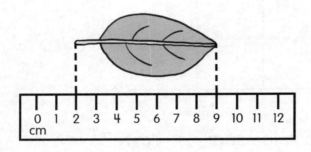

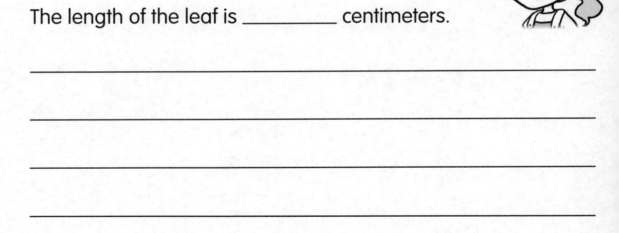

This ruler is smaller than in real life.

The length of the leaf is _____ centimeters.

_____

_____

_____

_____

_____

14.   Look at the bar model.
Write a real-world problem.

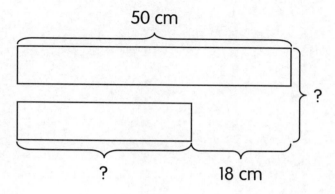

_____

_____

_____

_____

_____

Mass

PROBLEM SOLVING
Thinking Skills

Solve.
Show your work.

1.   The picture shows David's and Janet's mass four years ago.
     David has added 5 kilograms of mass.
     Janet has added 7 kilograms of mass.
     Who is heavier now?
     How much heavier?

_____ is _____ kilograms heavier than _____ .

2.   Look at the pictures.
Order the boxes from lightest to heaviest.

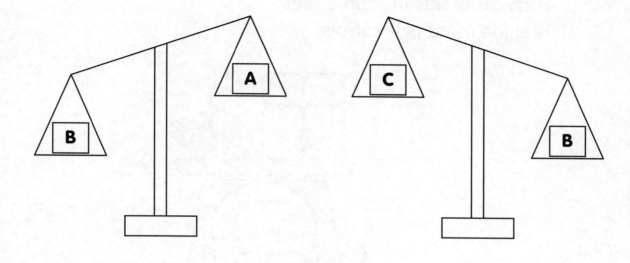

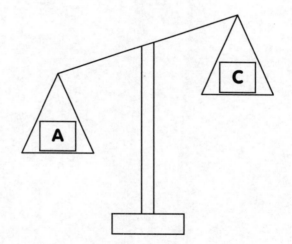

Box _____, Box _____, Box _____
      lightest

3.   Look at the picture.
Each ☐ is 50 grams.
Each carrot has the same mass.
Find the mass of 4 carrots.

The mass of 4 carrots is _____ grams.

Name: _____   **Date:** _____

Solve.
Show your work.

4.   Each watermelon has the same mass.
Find the total mass of 2 watermelons.

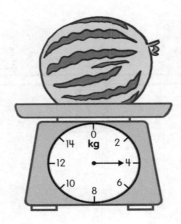

The total mass of 2 watermelons is _____ kilograms.

5. Each ☐ has a mass of 20 grams.
The books all have the same mass.
Find the mass of the toy car.

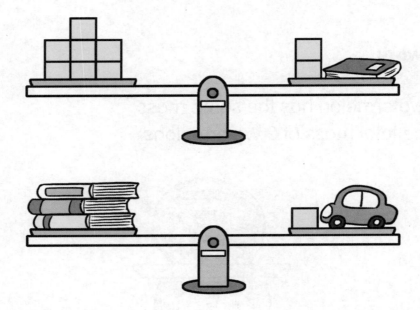

The mass of the toy car is _____ grams.

6. The mass of a metal cupboard is ✚ + ◯ + ☆ + ☆.
Find the mass of the cupboard.

☆ + ✚ + ◯ = 35 kilograms

☆ + ◯ = 30 kilograms

✚ + ✚ = ☆

The mass of the metal cupboard is _____ kilograms.

7. The total mass of two blocks of wood is 650 grams.
One block is 250 grams lighter than the other block.
Find the mass of each block of wood.

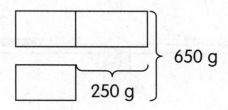

650 g

250 g

One block of wood has a mass of _____ grams.

The other block of wood has a mass of _____ grams.

8. The mass of each □ is 2 kilograms.
Find the mass of the vase.

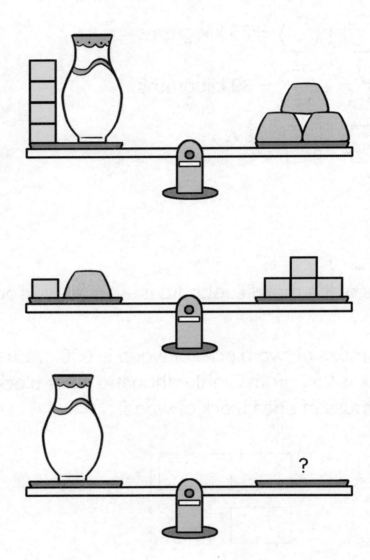

The mass of the vase is _____ kilograms.

PROBLEM SOLVING

Exploration

Solve.
Show your work.

9.

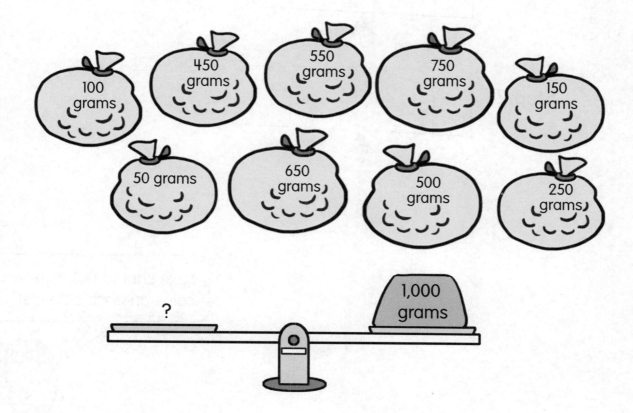

Which three bags will balance the 1,000 gram mass on the right?
List all possible answers.

10. Luke has four coins.
One coin is heavier than the other coins.
He uses a balance to find out which coin it is.
Draw the coins on the balances to show how Luke finds the answer.

Step 1

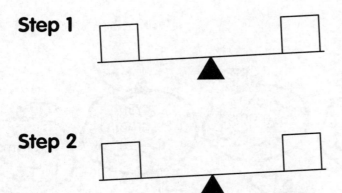

Step 2

Luke should balance two coins on each side first.

Journal Writing

Solve and explain.

11. Explain how you know which set is heavier.
How much heavier is the set?

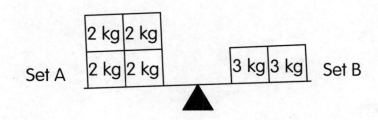

Set A | 2 kg 2 kg / 2 kg 2 kg   3 kg 3 kg | Set B

12. Write a real-world problem for the bar model.

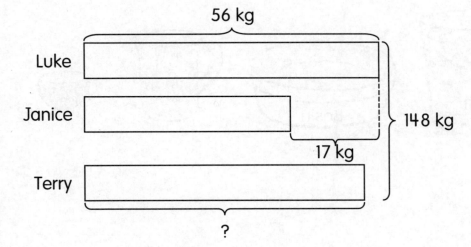

56 kg

Luke

Janice   148 kg

17 kg

Terry

?

CHAPTER 9 Volume

PROBLEM SOLVING

Thinking Skills

Solve.

Show your work.

1. The pail can hold two basins of water.
   Two jugs of water can fill up the basin.
   Three cups of water can fill up the jug.
   How many cups of water can the pail hold?

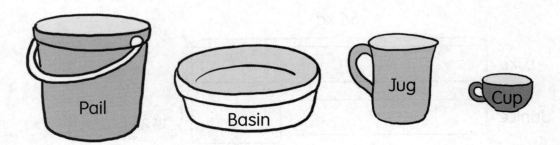

The pail can hold _____ cups of water.

2.   Three children are washing their bikes.
Roy uses 10 liters of water more than Peter.
Jill uses 9 liters of water less than Roy.
Peter uses 24 liters of water to wash his bike.
How much water do they use in all?

They use _____ liters of water in all.

3.   A tank contains 45 liters of water.
The tank can hold 85 liters of water when it is full.
Mr. Smith removes 3 pails of water from the tank.
Each pail holds 5 liters of water.
How many more liters of water will it take to fill the tank
completely?

_____ more liters of water will fill the tank completely.

PROBLEM SOLVING

Strategies

Solve.
Show your work.

4.   Paul has two cans of white paint.
He mixes them with 8 liters of yellow paint.
He uses 25 liters of the mixed paint to paint his house.
He has 3 liters of paint left.
How much white paint does Paul have at first?

Paul has _____ liters of white paint at first.

5.   The table shows the amount of water removed
from a tank every hour.
The tank had 50 liters of water at first.

Time	2 P.M.	3 P.M.	4 P.M.	5 P.M.	6 P.M.	7 P.M.	8 P.M.
Amount of water removed	1 liter	2 liters	3 liters	4 liters	5 liters	6 liters	7 liters

   a.   How much water will there be in the tank after 8 P.M.?

   There will be _____ liters of water in the tank.

   b.   How much water will there be in the tank after 10 P.M.?

   There will be _____ liters of water in the tank.

6.   Two hours ago, a tank had 15 liters of water.
Water was not removed from the tank.
5 liters of water is poured into the tank every hour.
How much water will be in the tank three hours from now?

There will be _____ liters of water in the tank three hours
from now.

PROBLEM SOLVING

Exploration

Solve.
Show your work.

7.   Tina has three pails of the same size.
        Each pail can hold 12 liters of water when full.
        Each pail contains a different amount of water now.

a. How can Tina get 7 liters of water from the three pails?

b. What other volumes of water can she get from the
        three pails?

Journal Writing

Write real-world problems.

8. Write a real-world problem that uses addition and subtraction.
Use the words to help you.

lemonade	in all	12 liters
7 liters	Ling	less than
Keith	how much	sell

9. Change one number in the problem.
The answer to the new problem should be:
20 cups of juice fill a jug.

4 cups of juice fill a glass.
7 glasses of juice fill a jug.
How many cups of juice fill a jug?

Answers

Chapter 1

Numbers to 1,000

1. Thinking Skill: Sequencing
   Solution: 193, 458, 496, 658, 867

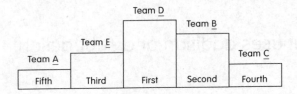

Team D — First
Team E — Third
Team B — Second
Team A — Fifth
Team C — Fourth

2. Thinking Skill: Sequencing
   Solution:

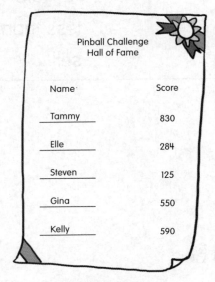

Pinball Challenge
Hall of Fame

Name	Score
Tammy	830
Elle	284
Steven	125
Gina	550
Kelly	590

3. Thinking Skill: Comparing
   Solution: 219
4. Thinking Skill: Comparing
   Solution: 549, 945
5. Strategy: Use a diagram
   Solution: 200
6. Strategy: Use a diagram
   Solution: 370
7. Strategy: Use a diagram
   Solution: 400

8. Strategy:
   Solution:

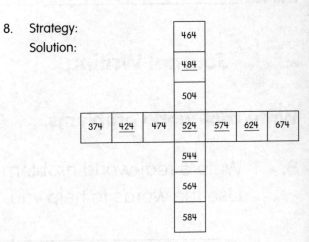

464
484
504
374 | 424 | 474 | 524 | 574 | 624 | 674
544
564
584

9. Strategy: Look for patterns
   Solution:

| 375 | ♡♡♡☆☆☆☆○○○ |

10. Strategy: Look for patterns
    Solution: 129 (For all other numbers, the first two digits add up to the last digit.)
11. 24 three-digit numbers are possible.
    147, 149, 174, 179, 194, 197,
    417, 419, 471, 479, 491, 497,
    714, 719, 741, 749, 791, 794,
    914, 917, 941, 947, 971 and 974.
12. The greatest three-digit number is <u>974</u>.
13. The smallest three-digit number is <u>147</u>.
14. 600 and 650; 900 and 950; 650 and 900
    Pattern 1:
    600 650 700 750 800 850
    Pattern 2:
    700 750 800 850 900 950
    Pattern 3:
    650 700 750 800 850 900
    Pattern 4:
    850 800 750 700 650 600
    Pattern 5:
    950 900 850 800 750 700
    Pattern 6:
    900 850 800 750 700 650
15. 2, 4, 3, 1

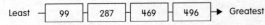

Least — 99 — 287 — 469 — 496 → Greatest

16. Answers vary.

Least — 88 — 472 — 507 — 540 → Greatest

17. Answers vary.
    For example: 75 more than 400 is 475.
18. Answers vary.
    For example: 125 more than 525 is 650.
19. 274, 375, 476, 577, 678
20. 99, 299, 307, 370, 901

Chapter 2

Addition up to 1,000

1. Thinking Skill: Comparing
   Solution: Color 315, 213

2. Thinking Skill: Comparing
   Solution: Color 193, 65, 136

3. Thinking Skill: Deduction
   Solution: a. Digit 1: 429
           Digit 2: 290
           Digit 3: 119
           Digit 4: 938
       b. 5803

4. Thinking Skill: Analyzing parts and whole
   Solution: $67 + $128 + $199 = $394
   Mrs. Thomas can buy the chair, bookcase, and couch.

5. Strategy: Work backwards
   Solution:

   ```
     1   1
   ( 2)  6  (9)
   +  6  6   6
   ─────────────
      9 (3)  5
   ```

6. Strategy: Work backwards
   Solution:

   ```
     1   1
   ( 4)  5   9
   +  4 (8) (9)
   ─────────────
      9  4   8
   ```

7. Strategy: Look for patterns
   Solution: 75 + 175, 95 + 155, 115 + 135
           250 + 250 + 250 + 55 = <u>805</u>

8. Strategy: Use a diagram
   Solution: 192 + 163 = 355
   She sells 355 bookmarks on Tuesday.
   192 + 355 + 34 = 581
   Mrs. Parker had <u>581</u> bookmarks at first.

9. Strategy: Use a diagram
   Solution: 80 + 72 = 152
   Samantha gives 152 seashells away.
   152 + 145 + 69 = 366
   Samantha had <u>366</u> seashells at first.

10. Strategy: Use a diagram
    Solution: 358 + 289 = 647
    Kathy has 647 baseball cards.
    647 + 127 = 774
    Jack had <u>774</u> baseball cards at first.

11. Trace in red the path from 172 to 384 to 439.
    172 + 384 + 439 = 995
    The greatest sum is <u>995</u>.

12. Accept any two answers that add up to 9.
    For example, 1 and 8, 2 and 7, or 3 and 6.

13. 137 + 486 = 623

14. 572 + 345 = 917

15. 25 + 75 = 100; 65 + 35 = 100; 45 + 55 = 100; 15 + 85 = 100
    25 + 75 + 65 + 35 + 45 + 55 + 15 + 85 = 100 + 100 + 100 + 100 = 400

16. Answers vary.
    For example,
    15, 35, 10, 40, 25, 25
    Group the numbers in pairs that add up to 50.
    15 + 35 = 50; 10 + 40 = 50; 25 + 25 = 50
    15 + 35 + 10 + 40 + 25 + 25 = 50 + 50 + 50
                                = 150

Chapter 3

Subtraction up to 1,000

1. Thinking Skill: Analyzing parts and whole
   Solution: 231

2. Thinking Skill: Analyzing parts and whole
   Solution: 583

3. Thinking Skill: Analyzing parts and whole
   Solution: 194

4. Thinking Skill: Analyzing parts and whole
   Solution: 319

5. Thinking Skill: Analyzing parts and whole
   Solution:

   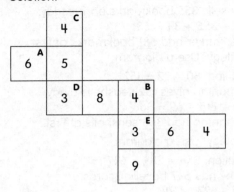

   <u>Down</u>

   B: <u>439</u> is 238 more than 201.
   C: 150 less that 603 is <u>453</u>.

   <u>Across</u>

   A: 425 − 360 = <u>65</u>
   D: 154 is <u>384</u> less than 538.
   E: 728 − <u>364</u> = 364

6. Thinking Skill: Analyzing parts and whole
   Solution: 131 − 48 − 68 = 15
   Peter gave Fraser <u>15</u> stickers.

7. Thinking Skill: Analyzing parts and whole
   Solution: 249 − 150 = 99
   There are 99 red bands.
   736 − 249 − 99 = 388
   The box contains <u>388</u> blue bands.

8. Strategy: Work backwards
   Solution:

9. Strategy: Look for patterns
   Solution:

   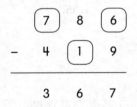

10. Strategy: Look for patterns
    Solution:

    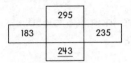

    235 − 183 = 52
    295 − 52 = 243
    The missing number is <u>243</u>.

11. Strategy: Make a list or guess and check
    Solution:
    a. 801, 245
    b. 801, 672

12. Strategy: Work backwards
    Solution: 495 − 85 − 95 = 315
    After adding the guppies, there are 315 fish.
    315 − 156 = 159
    <u>159</u> fish were in the pond at first.

13. Answers vary.
    For example, <u>4</u> hundreds <u>10</u> tens <u>100</u> ones

14. Answers vary.
    X + Y = 10
    For example, X = 1 and Y = 9; X = 2 and Y = 8

15. a. Sue keeps 45 marbles each time.
    b. 100 − 45 = 55
       Sue returns 55 marbles to Lee.
    c. 90 + 45 = 135
       Lee gave Sue 135 marbles.

16. Answers vary.

Chapter 4

Using Bar Models: Addition and Subtraction

1. Strategy: Use a diagram
   Solution:

   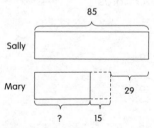

   85 − 29 = 56
   Mary has 56 stamps.
   56 − 15 = 41
   Mary has <u>41</u> stamps in the end.

2. Strategy: Use a diagram
   Solution:

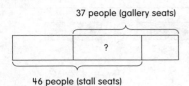

   46 + 37 = 83
   83 tickets are sold in all.
   83 − 59 = 24
   24 people buy tickets for both stall seats and gallery seats.

3. Strategy: Use a diagram
   Solution:

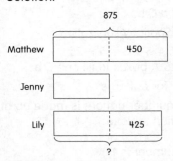

   875 − 450 = 425
   Jenny sells 425 pencils.
   425 + 425 = 850
   Lily sells <u>850</u> pencils.

4. Strategy: Use a diagram
   Solution:

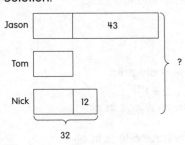

   32 − 12 = 20
   Tom collects 20 toys.
   20 + 43 = 63
   Jason collects 63 toys.
   63 + 20 + 32 = 115
   They collect <u>115</u> toys in all.

5. Strategy: Use a diagram
   Solution:

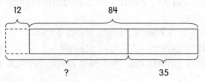

   84 − 35 = 49
   49 + 12 = 61
   Chelsea had <u>61</u> strawberries at first.

6. Strategy: Use a diagram
   Solution:

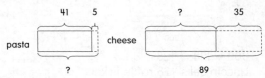

   41 + 5 = 46
   He had 46 packets of pasta at first.
   89 − 35 = 54
   He had 54 packets of cheese at first.
   46 + 54 = 100
   Adrian had 100 packets of pasta and cheese at first.

7. Strategy: Use a diagram
   Solution:

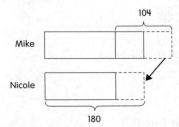

   52 + 52 = 104
   Mike gives Nicole 52 stamps.
   180 + 52 = 232
   Mike had 232 stamps at first.

8. Answers vary.
   For example,
   There are some marbles in three boxes, A, B, and C.
   There are 137 marbles in box A and 492 marbles in box B.
   There are a total of 800 marbles in boxes B and C.
   How many marbles are there in box C?

9. Answers vary.
For example,
Jenny scored 752 points in a mathematics competition.
Joel scored 149 less points than Jenny.
How many points did Joel score?
How many points did the two children score in all?

10.

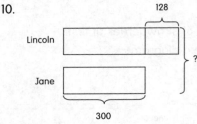

300 + 128 = 428
Lincoln sells 428 raffle tickets.
428 + 300 = 728
They sell 728 raffle tickets in all.

11.

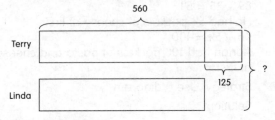

560 − 125 = 435
Linda has 435 books.
560 + 435 = 995
They have 995 books in all.

Chapter 5

Multiplication and Division

1. $5 \times 7 = \underline{35}$

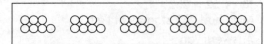

$7 \times 5 = \underline{35}$

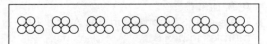

The two sentences have the factors in a different order.

2. Thinking Skill: Comparing
Solution:

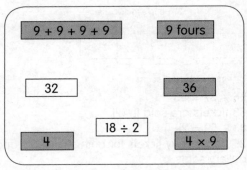

3. Thinking Skill: Spatial Visualization
Solution: $4 + 4 + 4 + 4 = 16$
<u>16</u> A boxes fill a C box.

4. Thinking Skill: Spatial Visualization
Solution: $5 + 5 + 5 + 5 + 5 = 25$
Gerald uses <u>25</u> A boxes to fill one C box.

5. Strategy: Look for patterns
Solution: The number pattern is made up of the multiplication table of 7.
$7 \times 2 = 14$
The missing number is <u>14</u>.

6. Strategy: Guess and check
Solution:
$\underline{2} \times \underline{3} = \underline{6}$ or $\underline{3} \times \underline{2} = \underline{6}$
$\underline{2} \times \underline{8} = \underline{16}$ or $\underline{8} \times \underline{2} = \underline{16}$
$\underline{3} \times \underline{7} = \underline{21}$ or $\underline{7} \times \underline{3} = \underline{21}$

7. Strategy: Make suppositions
Solution:

☆ = 2   ☾ = 4   △ = 16

8. Strategy: Use a diagram
Solution: $4 \times 2 = 8$
The ducks have 8 legs in all.
$3 \times 2 = 6$
The chickens have 6 legs in all.
$30 - 8 - 6 = 16$
The cows have 16 legs in all.
$16 \div 4 = 4$
The farmer has <u>4</u> cows.

9. Strategy: Solve part of the problem
Solution: $28 + 2 = 30$
🍐 = 30
$30 \div 6 = 5$
🍎 = 5
$5 \times 3 = 15$
🍎 = 15

10. She can divide the paper among the files in <u>six</u> ways.
    1. 2 × 12, 24 ÷ 2
    2. 3 × 8, 24 ÷ 3
    3. 4 × 6, 24 ÷ 4
    4. 12 × 2, 24 ÷ 12
    5. 8 × 3, 24 ÷ 8
    6. 6 × 4, 24 ÷ 6

11. Answers vary.
For example,
6 cars, 2 tricycles, 1 bicycle (combination with the most number of cars possible)
1 car, 8 tricycles, 2 bicycles (combination with the most number of tricycles possible)
1 car, 2 tricycles, 11 bicycles (combination with the most number of bicycles possible)

12. Answers vary.
For example,
3 × 8: The answer is twice that of 3 × 4. A related division sentence is 24 ÷ 3 = 8.
12 ÷ 4: A related multiplication sentence is 3 × 4 = 12.

13. 2 × 4 = 8
The rabbits have 8 legs in all.
14 − 8 = 6
The chickens have 6 legs in all.
6 ÷ 2 = 3
There are <u>3</u> chickens.

Chapter 6

Multiplication Tables of 2, 5, and 10

1. Thinking Skill: Deduction
Solution:

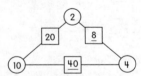

2. Thinking Skill: Deduction
Solution:

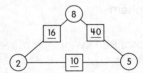

3. Thinking Skill: Identifying patterns and relationships
Solution:

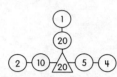

4. Thinking Skill: Identifying patterns and relationships
Solution:

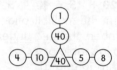

5. Answers vary.
For example,

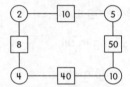

6. Thinking Skill: Deduction
Solution: Answers vary.
For example,

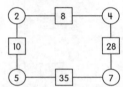

7. Thinking Skill: Deduction
Solution:

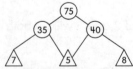

8. Thinking Skill: Deduction
Solution:

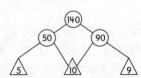

9. Strategy: Guess and check or make a supposition
Solution: 20 × 2 = 40
       40 ÷ 5 = <u>8</u>

10. Strategy: Guess and check or make
a supposition
Solution: $3 \times 10 = 30$
$30 \div 5 = \underline{6}$

11.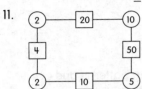

12. Strategy: Look for patterns
Solution: **30**, <u>12</u>, **25**, <u>10</u>, **20**, <u>8</u>, **15**, <u>6</u>, **10**, <u>4</u>, **5**, <u>2</u>
The numbers in **bold** form the multiplication table of 5, while the numbers that are <u>underlined</u> form the multiplication table of 2.
Therefore, the answers are 10 and 10.

13. Strategy: Use a diagram
Solution: $10 \times 10 = 100$
The cars are 100 meters long in all.
$9 \times 2 = 18$
The links are 18 meters long in all.
$100 + 18 = 118$
The length of the train is <u>118</u> meters.

14–15.
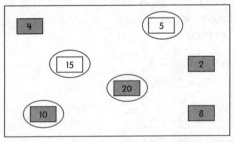

16. The numbers that are both shaded and circled are 10 and 20.

17. Answers vary.
Common multiples of 2 and 5 will be both shaded and circled.
For example,
if the five numbers are 102, 110, 124, 130, and 142, 110 and 130 will be both shaded and circled.

18. $20 \div 4 = 5$
The machine multiplies each number by 5.
The numbers produced are <u>15</u>, <u>25</u>, <u>35</u>, and <u>45</u>.

19. Yes, she can divide them equally into groups of 2 because 24 is divisible by 2.
No, she cannot divide them equally into groups of 5 because 24 is not divisible by 5.

20. There are 7 chickens. Each chicken has 2 legs.
There are 14 legs in all.

21. $2 \times 9 = 18$, or $20 + 9 = 29$

22. $7 \times 5 = 3 \times 5 + 4 \times 5$

Chapter 7

Metric Measurement of Length

1. Thinking Skill: Comparing
Solution: 14

2. Thinking Skill: Comparing
Solution: 3; 11

3. Thinking Skill: Analyzing parts and whole
Solution: $5 + 8 + 19 = 32$

4. Thinking Skill: Analyzing parts and whole
Solution: $42 + 18 + 40 = 100$
The lengths of the pieces are <u>42</u> centimeters, <u>18</u> centimeters, and <u>40</u> centimeters.

5. Thinking Skill: Comparing
Solution: $90 - 8 = 82$
Kate is 82 centimeters tall.
$82 + 24 = 106$
Raymond is 106 centimeters tall.
$106 + 82 = 188$
Their total height is <u>188</u> centimeters.

6. Strategy: Work backward
Solution:
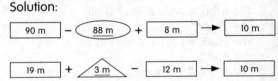

7. Strategy: Use a diagram
Solution:
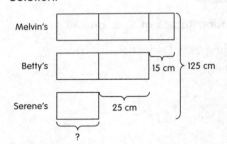

$125 - 25 - 25 - 15 = 60$
$60 \div 3 = 20$
Serene's house is <u>20</u> centimeters tall.

8. Strategy: Look for patterns
Solution: $5 - 3 = 2$
For every 5 meters that Ben swims, he moves only 2 meters up the river.
$12 \div 2 = 6$
He swam 6 sets of 5 meters.
$6 \times 5 = 30$
Ben swims <u>30</u> meters in all.

9. Strategy: Look for patterns

Solution: $80 \div 10 = 8$
There are 8 meters between each light.
$8 \times 4 = 32$
The sixth garden light is 32 meters away from the second.

10. Strategy: Simplify the problem

Solution: $250 + 50 = 300$
The total length of the two pieces of wood is 300 centimeters.
$300 \div 3 = 100$
The shorter piece of wood is 100 centimeters long.

11. Answers vary.
For example,
Length of paper clip: 8 cm – 3 cm = 5 cm
Length of eraser: 10 cm – 2 cm = 8 cm
Difference in length: 8 cm – 5 cm = 3 cm

Comparing the length on the left, the eraser is 1 cm longer.
Comparing the length on the right, the eraser is 2 cm longer.
1 cm + 2 cm = 3 cm
So, the eraser is 3 cm longer.

12. (In any order) 12 + 12 + 15 + 15 + 15 = 69
The shortest distance the snail can crawl is 69 centimeters.

13. $9 - 2 = 7$
The length of the leaf is 7 centimeters.

14. Answers vary.
For example,
Annie has a piece of ribbon 50 centimeters long. Her sister has another piece of ribbon that is 18 centimeters shorter.
What is the length of her sister's ribbon?
What is the total length of the two ribbons?

Chapter 8

Mass

1. Thinking Skill: Comparing

Solution: $40 + 5 = 45$
David's mass is now 45 kilograms.
$20 + 7 = 27$
Janet's mass is now 27 kilograms.
$45 - 27 = 18$
The difference in their mass now is 18 kilograms.
David is 18 kilograms heavier than Janet.

2. Thinking Skill: Sequencing

Solution: Box C, Box A, Box B

3. Thinking Skill: Analyzing parts and whole

Solution:
$50 + 50 + 50 + 50 + 50 + 50 = 300$
The total mass of the blocks is 300 grams.
$700 - 300 = 400$
Two carrots weigh 400 grams.
$400 + 400 = 800$
The mass of 4 carrots is 800 grams.

4. Strategy: Use a diagram

Solution: The mass of one watermelon is 4 kilograms.
$2 \times 4 = 8$
The total mass of 2 watermelons is 8 kilograms.

5. Strategy: Solve part of the problem

Solution:
$20 + 20 + 20 + 20 + 20 + 20 + 20 = 140$
$140 - 20 - 20 = 100$
The mass of the book is 100 grams.
$100 + 100 + 100 = 300$
$300 - 20 = 280$
The mass of the toy car is 280 grams.

6. Strategy: Simplify the problem

Solution: ⬚ = 35 – 30 = 5 kilograms

☆ = 5 + 5 = 10 kilograms

◯ = 30 – 10 = 20 kilograms

$5 + 20 + 10 + 10 = 45$
The mass of the metal cupboard is 45 kilograms.

7. Strategy: Use a diagram

Solution:

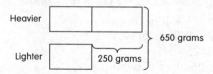

$650 - 250 = 400$
$400 \div 2 = 200$
One block of wood has a mass of 200 grams.
$200 + 250 = 450$
The other block of wood has a mass of 450 grams.

8. Strategy: Simplify the problem

Solution:

⬚⬚⬚ = 4 × 2 = 8 kilograms

▲ + ⬚ = 8 kilograms

▲ = 8 – 2 = 6 kilograms

⬚ = 6 × 3 = 18 kilograms

$18 - 8 = 10$
The mass of the vase is 10 kilograms.

9. 750 grams, 150 grams, 100 grams, or
   650 grams, 250 grams, 100 grams, or
   500 grams, 450 grams, 50 grams

10. The first balance shows two coins on each
    side, one side is heavier.
    The second balance shows one coin on each
    side, one side is heavier.

11. The side of the scale with the heavier set
    will be lower.
    $4 \times 2 = 8$
    Set A is 8 kilograms
    $2 \times 3 = 6$
    Set B is 6 kilograms.
    $8 - 6 = 2$
    The difference in their mass is 2 kilograms.

12. Answers vary.
    For example,
    Luke's mass is 56 kilograms.
    Janice's mass is 17 kilograms less than Luke's.
    The total mass of Luke, Janice, and Terry is
    148 kilograms.
    What is Terry's mass?

Chapter 9

Volume

1. Thinking Skill: Analyzing parts and whole
   Solution: $3 \times 2 = 6$
   6 cups of water are needed to fill up a basin.
   $6 \times 2 = 12$
   The pail can hold <u>12</u> cups of water.

2. Thinking Skill: Analyzing parts and whole
   Solution: $24 + 10 = 34$
   Roy uses 34 liters of water.
   $34 - 9 = 25$
   Jill uses 25 liters of water.
   $24 + 34 + 25 = 83$
   They use <u>83</u> liters of water in all.

3. Thinking Skill: Analyzing parts and whole
   Solution: $3 \times 5 = 15$
   Mr. Smith removes 15 liters of water.
   $45 - 15 = 30$
   The tank now contains 30 liters of water.
   $85 - 30 = 55$
   <u>55</u> more liters of water will fill the tank
   completely.

4. Strategy: Work backwards
   Solution: $25 + 3 = 28$
   He has 28 liters of mixed paint.
   $28 - 8 = 20$
   Paul has <u>20</u> liters of white paint at first.

5. Strategy: Look for patterns
   Solution:
   a. $1 + 2 + 3 + 4 + 5 + 6 + 7 = 28$
      28 liters of water is removed from 2 P.M. to
      8 P.M.
      $50 - 28 = 22$
      There will be <u>22</u> liters of water in the tank.
   b. $22 - 8 - 9 = 5$
      There will be <u>5</u> liters of water in the tank.

6. Strategy: Look for patterns
   Solution: $15 + 5 + 5 = 25$
   There is 25 liters of water in the tank now.
   $25 + 5 + 5 + 5 = 40$
   There will be <u>40</u> liters of water in the tank
   three hour from now.

7. a. Answers vary.
      For example,
      From the 3-liter pail, pour 2 liters of water
      into the 10-liter pail and the remaining 1 liter
      of water into the 6-liter pail to get 7 liters of
      water.
   b. Answers vary.

8. Answers vary.
   For example,
   Ling sells 12 liters of lemonade.
   Keith sells 7 liters less lemonade than Ling
   does.
   How much lemonade do they sell in all?

9. 4 cups of juice fill a glass.
   <u>5</u> glasses of juice fill a jug.
   How many cups of juice fill a jug?